To

_____

_____

_____

From

_____

_____

_____

Hope Helps, from Nana

Secrets for a Better Life

in Easy Words from Scripture

Rosie Clandos

Dedicated

To my grandchildren Taya, Isaac, and Gracie,

And to my future great grandchildren

For grandchildren of all ages

Special thanks to June Abramian for insightful editing

Contents

Hope Helps, from Nana

Get Ready

Pray Anyway

There are lots of different ways to pray. Talk to God. Sing to God. Write to God. Or you can read the letters or songs other people wrote to God. You can pray when you walk, work, play, exercise, or rest.

You can praise God, thank him, or apologize to God. You can ask for what you need or what others need. If you're upset, you can pray anyway.

Finding Hope

When you pray, you naturally hope that God will answer your prayers. Feeling hopeful will help you find solutions to problems. But there may be times when you feel bad. You may not feel hopeful.

To help us feel hope, we can thank God for something, anything – for small things, for big things, for lots of things. Being grateful helps us to have hopeful thoughts. God made our brains to work that way. And guess what? Hope is catchy. It's contagious. When we have hope, other people might catch our hopeful feelings, too.

Yes, No, Wait, or Keep Praying

Sometimes our prayers are answered the way we want. Sometimes they're not. Sometimes they're answered later or in unusual ways. Still, we can ask God questions and honestly tell him how we feel. Even when we're upset.

We may change our prayers. We may think more about our requests. We can do what we know is right. We can believe that God is good, and he will care for us.

When we look around for the blessings that God already gave us, we may feel more hopeful or patient. But sometimes, we may have to keep praying. We can refuse to quit. We can be persistent.

Say it. Picture it. Write it. Act it. Repeat it!

Reading Scripture is often like learning new ways to think or act. Just like any other lesson, we can remember a scripture verse better when we repeat it while we do something physical, like walk or run or draw or write.

Can't Forgive? Try this!

God tells people to love each other, and to forgive those who hurt us. But there are times when we feel like we can't forgive! What can we do then?

We can do something different: We can bless them. If someone has been unkind, we can ask God to bless that person with kindness, so they will be kind to us and others. If someone has told lies about us, we can ask God to bless that person with honesty.

We can bless anyone with any good thing to help them act better. After we *give* a blessing to *for-give* someone, we may feel happier and healthier. And maybe they will, too.

Stick Around

God wants us to stay close to him all day long. That means talking to him and listening to our conscience. Some people say that our conscience is God's voice. Other people say that our conscience is a sense, or a feeling, about what is right and wrong. The point is this: Do what you know is right. Be kind. Be fair. Walk humbly with God.

Loving people, forgiving others and staying close to God are all ways to help us feel happier and healthier.

Prayer Works

I don't have all the answers, but I do know that God loves us, and that prayer works. Prayer helps to connect us with God. And that's a good thing for you and others.

I believe God made our bodies. And our bodies work better when we care for our ourselves, and when we're loving, forgiving, and staying close to God.

Choices

Jesus gave us examples of how to be loving and forgiving. God allows people to make choices, and he wants people to make good choices. But some people make bad ones.

Accidents, wars, and bad things happen. Illness and mistakes happen. But we can choose to keep looking for something good. And when we look, we will find it.

Can or Will

In this book, there are many sentences that start with the words "I can". Saying "I can" is helpful, but when I need to feel extra strong, I firmly say the words *"I will"*. It's your choice: You pick it: "I can" or "I will".

Making Sense

Scriptures were written a long time ago and in different ways –
as stories, poems, facts, and more. The verses in this book may
be part of a bigger or unexpected story. Still, they make sense for
our purposes. They're based on faith, love, and courage. Nana's
words are based on my experience and research. Adults can read
more in my book ***Turn on Hope Street: Stories, Faith and
Neuroscience.***

Together for Good

One last thing: You are not alone. God is with you, and he loves
you. He wants to help you have a good life. We all want that for
you, dear one.

Love,

Nana

Anger

Scripture: A gentle answer turns away wrath, but a harsh word stirs up anger. Proverb 15:1 (NIV)

Nana's words: I can speak kindly. If I'm rude or unkind, problems can happen. I can refuse to be rude and get in trouble. I can be honest and respectful when I say how I feel.

Write comments or draw. When or where to use this verse?

Scripture: Don't sin by letting anger control you. Don't let the sun go down while you are still angry. Ephesians 4:26 (NLT)

Nana's words: I understand it's normal to be angry. I can honestly talk to God about what's making me mad. He helps me to solve problems and forgive people. I can trust God and sleep better.

Write comments or draw. Use this verse: When? Where?

Scripture: Whoever is patient has great understanding, but one who is quick-tempered displays folly. Proverb 14:29 (NIV)

Nana's words: When I act patiently, I can think better. I feel smarter. I refuse to get angry quickly and make mistakes that hurt me or others.

Write comments or draw. Use this verse: When? Where?

Scripture: My dear brothers and sisters, take note of this: Everyone should be quick to listen, slow to speak and slow to become angry. James 1:19 (NIV)

Nana's words: When I'm angry, I can take time to listen and think before I speak. I can ask questions to help me understand more.

Write comments or draw. Use this verse: When? Where?

Scripture: Losing your temper is foolish; ignoring an insult is smart. Proverb 12:16 (CEV)

Nana's words: I don't have to lose my temper. I can close my mouth if I want to say something mean. And I can walk away if I want to hit or hurt someone. I can refuse to lose my temper and hurt someone or myself.

Write comments or draw. Use this verse: When? Where?

Scripture: Fathers, do not provoke your children to anger by the way you treat them. Rather, bring them up with the discipline and instruction that comes from the Lord. Ephesians 6:4 (ESV)

Nana's words: I know everyone makes mistakes. If my dad or mom is unkind or unfair, I can quietly pray and bless them with kindness and wisdom. I can choose to be kind to my family. I know that kindness is catchy.

Write comments or draw. Use this verse: When? Where?

Apologize

Scripture: If we confess our sins to God, he can always be trusted to forgive us and take away our sins. 1 John 1:9 (CEV)

Nana's words: I can talk to God about things I've done wrong. God always forgives me. I know he loves me and that helps me act better.

Write comments or draw. Use this verse: When? Where?

Scripture: Confess your sins to each other and pray for each other so that you may be healed. The earnest prayer of a righteous person has great power and produces wonderful results. James 5:16 (NLT)

Nana's words: I can apologize to people who I've hurt, and I pray for them. When I apologize, good things often happen. I can feel peaceful, stronger, and wiser.

Write comments or draw. Use this verse: When? Where?

Scripture: Be kind to each other, tenderhearted, forgiving one another, just as God through Christ has forgiven you. Ephesians 4:32 (NIV)

Nana's words: I can be kind and tender to my family, friends, and others. God forgives me. So, I can *for-give* others and *give* them a blessing.

Write comments or draw. Use this verse: When? Where?

Ask

Scripture: Stay joined to me and let my teachings become part of you. Then you can pray for whatever you want, and your prayer will be answered. John 15:7 (CEV)

Nana's words: I can stay close to God and talk to him often. I can learn and pray for what I want. I know that God will say yes, no, wait or keep praying.

Write comments or draw. Use this verse: When? Where?

Scripture: And we are confident that he hears us whenever we ask for anything that pleases him. 1 John 5:14 (NLT)

Nana's words: I know that God hears me when I pray. I can ask for things that are good and will help me or others.

Write comments or draw. Use this verse: When? Where?

Scripture: I tell you, you can pray for anything, and if you believe that you've received it, it will be yours. Mark 11:24 (NLT)

Nana's words: I know I can ask for anything. And I know God wants me to ask for things that are good or helpful. I believe God can provide what I need now or later.

Write comments or draw. Use this verse: When? Where?

Scripture: When you are praying, first forgive anyone you are holding a grudge against, so that your Father in heaven will forgive you your sins, too. Mark 11:25 (NLT)

Nana's words: If someone has hurt me, I can give them a blessing so they act better. That helps me to forgive. Then I can trust God to forgive me for hurting others or myself.

Write comments or draw. Use this verse: When? Where?

Scripture: But when you ask for something, you must have faith and not doubt. Anyone who doubts is like an ocean wave tossed around in a storm. James 1:6 (CEV)

Nana's words: I can trust God to help me. I can thank him now. I will look for his little blessings or big blessings. I can refuse to doubt and worry. I believe that God can provide what I need or what my family needs.

Write comments or draw. Use this verse: When? Where?

Scripture: Keep on asking, and you will receive what you ask for. Keep on seeking, and you will find. Keep on knocking, and the door will be opened for you. For everyone who asks, receives. Everyone who seeks, find. And to everyone who knocks, the door will be opened. Matthew 7:7 (NLT)

Nana's words: I can keep asking and looking until I find what I need. I can decide not to nag my parents, but I can keep talking to God. I know that God will help me in some way, or through some person, now or later.

Write comments or draw. Use this verse: When? Where?

Bad Habits

Scripture: I can do all things through him who strengthens me. Philippians 4:13 (ESV)

Nana's words: I can ask God to help me break habits that aren't good for me. God can strengthen me. I am strong with God.

Write comments or draw. Use this verse: When? Where?

Scripture: Encourage the young men to be self-controlled. Titus 2:6 (NIV)

Nana's words: I can encourage myself and others to act and speak with self-control. We support each other.

Write comments or draw. Use this verse: When? Where?

Scripture: The temptations in your life are no different from what others experience. And God is faithful. He will not allow the temptation to be more than you can stand. When you are tempted, he will show you a way out so that you can endure. 1 Corinthians 10:13 (NLT)

Nana's words: I know everyone gets tempted to do wrong things. When I'm tempted, I can look for ways to distract myself or get away. I can find ways to protect myself from temptation and problems.

Write comments or draw. Use this verse: When? Where?

Scripture: All athletes are disciplined in their training. They do it to win a prize that will fade away, but we do it for an eternal prize. So, I run with purpose in every step. 1 Corinthians 9:25 (NLT)

Nana's words: I can build my self-control. I get many benefits from acting with self-control. Some of those benefits happen now, others happen later. I can focus on my goals that are good and healthy.

Write comments or draw. Use this verse: When? Where?

Scripture: Confess your sins to each other and pray for each other so that you may be healed. The earnest prayer of a righteous person has great power and produces wonderful results. James 5:16 (NLT)

Nana's words: I honestly talk to God about habits that aren't good for me. I can pray and get help from wise people.

Write comments or draw. Use this verse: When? Where?

Scripture: Put on all the armor that God gives, so you can defend yourself against the devil's tricks. Ephesians 6:11 (CEV)

Nana's words: I can do the special things that protect me. I remember that God loves me. I ask for help. I can tell the truth and act peacefully. I can use helpful Scripture verses and trust God. I thank God for what he's going to do.

Write comments or draw. Use this verse: When? Where?

Bullying

Scripture: Be strong and courageous. Do not be afraid or terrified of them, for the Lord your God goes with you. He will never leave you or forsake you. Deuteronomy 31:6 (NIV)

Nana's words: I am confident. I can ignore or walk away from mean kids. I can ask God to give me ideas for safety. I can get help from wise people. I know God is with me. I can find kind friends.

Write comments or draw. Use this verse: When? Where?

Scripture: For God gave us a spirit not of fear but of power, love, and self-control. 2 Timothy 1:7 (ESV)

Nana's words: I can practice self-control when someone is mean. I have God's power to help me. I can ignore lies and tell myself the truth: I am loved by God. I am precious. I can treat myself kindly.

Write comments or draw. Use this verse: When? Where?

Scripture: Do not let any unwholesome talk come out of your mouths, but only what is helpful for building others up according to their needs, that it may benefit those who listen. Ephesians 4:29 (NIV)

Nana's words: I can ask for help from my parents or others if I'm bullied. I can encourage my friends to be strong. I can treat others the way I want to be treated.

__Write comments or draw. Use this verse: When? Where?__

Scripture: "Do not seek revenge or bear a grudge against anyone among your people, but love your neighbor as yourself. I am the Lord." Leviticus 19:18 (NLT)

Nana's words: If I've been hurt, I can refuse to get even with the bully. I can keep away from them. I can refuse to be mean. I treat myself with respect. I can be kind and loving to myself.

__Write comments or draw. Use this verse: When? Where?__

Cheating

Scripture: People with integrity walk safely, but those who follow crooked paths will be exposed. Proverb 10:9 (NLT)

Nana's words: I can refuse to cheat. I want to be honest and safe. I don't want to be embarrassed or get a bad grade later.

Write comments or draw. Use this verse: When? Where?

Scripture: Do to others as you would have them do to you. Luke 6:1 (NIV)

Nana's words: I don't want anyone to steal my money or schoolwork. So, I can refuse to cheat or steal from anyone.

Write comments or draw. Use this verse: When? Where?

Scripture: If you are faithful in little things, you will be faithful in large ones. But if you are dishonest in little things, you won't be honest with greater responsibilities. Luke 16:10 (NLT)

Nana's words: I can be honest about little things. Then I'll be stronger and able to be honest about bigger things. I can refuse to lie and cheat.

Write comments or draw. Use this verse: When? Where?

Scripture: You shall not steal; you shall not deal falsely; you shall not lie to one another. Leviticus 19:11 (ESV)

Nana's words: I am strong and smart. I can refuse to lie or steal or cheat. I can study and get help with my work.

Write comments or draw. Use this verse: When? Where?

Chores

Scripture: I can do all things through him who strengthens me. Philippians 4:13 (ESV)

Nana's words: I ask God for help so I can do my chores and schoolwork. He can give me good ways to think and work. I can do one task at a time and then encourage myself.

__Write comments or draw. Use this verse: When? Where?__

Scripture: Do all things without grumbling or disputing. Philippians 2:14 (ESV)

Nana's words: I can feel better when I do my chores and schoolwork without complaining. I can refuse to make myself feel bad now or later by arguing. I am patient and kind to myself and my parents. I think of good ways to make my chores and schoolwork fun.

__Write comments or draw. Use this verse: When? Where?__

Scripture: Children, obey your parents in the Lord, for this is right. Ephesians 6:1 (NIV)

Nana's words: I know what is right, and I can do what is right. I can obey my mom and dad.

Write comments or draw. Use this verse: When? Where?

Scripture: Each will have to bear his own load. Galatians 6:5 (ESV)

Nana's words: I can do my work at school and at home. I can refuse to make others do my work for me. I feel good when I am reliable and responsible. I encourage myself while I work.

Write comments or draw. Use this verse: When? Where?

Comfort

Scripture: Come near to God and he will come near to you. James 4:8 (NIV)

Nana's words: I talk with God or write or sing to him. I can think about God being close to me in my home, at school, and outside. I believe that God is near me. He is with me.

Write comments or draw. Use this verse: When? Where?

Scripture: A father to the fatherless, a defender of widows, is God in his holy dwelling. Psalm 68:5 (NIV)

Nana's words: I can imagine that God is with me. When I feel lonely or upset, I can think about him helping me, directing me, or defending me.

Write comments or draw. Use this verse: When? Where?

Scripture: Though my father and mother forsake me, the Lord will receive me. Psalm 27:10 (NIV)

Nana's words: Even if my family or friends are not with me, I know that God is always with me. I can talk to him, and he will comfort me.

<u>*Write comments or draw. Use this verse: When? Where?*</u>

Compassion

Scripture: Be kind to one another, tenderhearted, forgiving one another, as God in Christ has forgiven you. Ephesians 4:32 (ESV)

Nana's words: I can be kind and tender. When people are sick or upset, they may be grouchy or afraid. I can choose to pray and bless people. I am kind and forgiving.

Write comments or draw. Use this verse: When? Where?

Scripture: Treat others as you want them to treat you. This is what the Law and the Prophets are all about. Matthew 7:12 (CEV)

Nana's words: I can treat people with compassion, in the same way I want to be treated. I can remember there have been times when I felt bad or acted bad.

Write comments or draw. Use this verse: When? Where?

Scripture: If anyone has the world's goods and sees his brother in need, yet closes his heart against him, how does God's love abide in him? 1 Thessalonians 5:11 (ESV)

Nana's words: I can try to help people in need. I can ask God about what I should do. But if I can't help, I can pray for them.

Write comments or draw. Use this verse: When? Where?

Courage

Scripture: This is my command – be strong and courageous! Do not be afraid or discouraged. For the Lord your God is with you wherever you go. Joshua 1:9 (NLT)

Nana's words: I am strong and courageous! I can refuse to be afraid. I can trust God. He is with me right here and wherever I go.

Write comments or draw. Use this verse: When? Where?

Scripture: For God gave us a spirit *not* of fear but of power and love and self-control. 2 Timothy 17 (ESV)

Nana's words: I know that God loves me and gives me power to do what I must do. I can have self-control and act with kindness.

Write comments or draw. Use this verse: When? Where?

Scripture: Wait for the Lord; be strong, and let your heart take courage; wait for the Lord! Psalm 27:14 (ESV)

Nana's words: I can take deep breaths and imagine that God is filling me with courage. As I wait for what I need, God makes me strong.

Write comments or draw. Use this verse: When? Where?

Depression

Scripture: When his people pray for help, he listens and rescues them from their troubles. Psalm 34:17 (CEV)

Nana's words: When I feel *de-pressed*, I can *ex-press* my feelings to God. I can talk, whisper, write, cry, hum, or get angry. I can move, walk, or exercise. I ask God and others for help. I look for their help. I thank God for little blessings.

Write comments or draw. Use this verse: When? Where?

Scripture: Don't be afraid, for I am with you. Don't be discouraged, for I am your God. I can strengthen you and help you. I can hold you up with my victorious right hand. Isaiah 41:10 (NLT)

Nana's words: When I am afraid or discouraged, I can choose to believe God will help me. He makes me strong when I thank him for his blessings.

Write comments or draw. Use this verse: When? Where?

Scripture: For I know the plans I have for you, says the Lord. They are plans for good and not for disaster, to give you a future and a hope. Jeremiah 29:11 (NLT)

Nana's words: I can choose to believe God wants me to have hope and a good future. I can refuse to believe that things are hopeless. I believe God can give me hope. I can look for hope and find it, little by little.

Write comments or draw. Use this verse: When? Where?

Scripture: You have turned my sorrow into joyful dancing. No longer am I sad and wearing sackcloth. Psalm 30:11 (CEV)

Nana's words: God can help me feel good again. Every day, I do things – even tiny things – to help me feel better. I can exercise or dance even when I don't feel happy. I can talk or write or cry to God. I ask for help from others. I am getting stronger every day.

Write comments or draw. Use this verse: When? Where?

Encourage

Scripture: The Lord himself goes before you and will be with you. He will never leave you nor forsake you. Do not be afraid. Do not be discouraged. Deuteronomy 31:8 (NIV)

Nana's words: I feel encouraged knowing that God is always with me. Discouragement doesn't fix anything. I can refuse to be discouraged. I can trust God.

Write comments or draw. Use this verse: When? Where?

Scripture: Encourage each other and build each other up, just as you are already doing. 1 Thessalonians 5:11 (NLT)

Nana's words: I can feel good when I encourage my family and friends. I can continue to be encouraging.

Write comments or draw. Use this verse: When? Where?

Scripture: Let us think of ways to motivate one another to acts of love and good works. Hebrews 10:24 (NLT)

Nana's words: I can think of ways to encourage myself and others. I help people or encourage my family to help others.

Write comments or draw. Use this verse: When? Where?

Scripture: Even though I walk through the darkest valley, I can fear no evil, for you are with me. Your rod and your staff, they comfort me. Psalm 23:4 (NIV)

Nana's words: Even though I may be frightened or discouraged, I can remember that God is with me. He will comfort me and encourage me. I can do things to keep myself safe.

Write comments or draw. Use this verse: When? Where?

Failure

Scripture: I can do all things though him who strengthens me. Philippians 4:13 (ESV)

Nana's words: When things go wrong, I can get strength from God.

Write comments or draw. Use this verse: When? Where?

Scripture: I know the plans I have for you, declares the Lord, plans to prosper you and not to harm you, plans to give you hope and a future. Jeremiah 29:11 (NIV)

Nana's words: I know God wants good things for me. He can give me the hope and the help to solve my problems.

Write comments or draw. Use this verse: When? Where?

Scripture: Our Lord, we belong to you. We tell you what worries us, and you won't let us fall. Psalm 55:22 (CEV)

Nana's words: I can talk to God about things that went wrong. I can refuse to treat myself badly or say mean things about myself. I learn from my mistakes. I think of ways to get smarter.

Write comments or draw. Use this verse: When? Where?

Fear

Scripture: Anxious hearts are very heavy, but a word of encouragement does wonders. Proverb 12:25 (TLB)

Nana's words: When I feel scared or worried, I can encourage myself. Encouraging words can make me feel good and help others. If I worry a lot, I can say lots of encouraging words. I can ask for help.

Write comments or draw. Use this verse: When? Where?

Scripture: For God gave us a spirit *not* of fear but of power and love and self-control. 2 Timothy 1:7 (ESV)

Nana's words: I can use the power, love, and self-control that God has given me. With God's power, I can speak and act with courage.

Write comments or draw. Use this verse: When? Where?

Scripture: Do not be anxious for anything; but in every situation, by prayer and petition, with thanksgiving, present your requests to God. Philippians 4:6 (NIV)

Nana's words: I can ask God for what I need today. Then I thank him, even before my prayers are answered. If I worry again, I can talk to him again and thank him for his help.

Write comments or draw. Use this verse: When? Where?

Scripture: Do not fear, for I am with you; do not be dismayed, for I am your God. I can strengthen you and help you; I can uphold you with my righteous right hand. Isaiah 41:10 (NIV)

Nana's words: I can trust that God is with me. I can refuse to be afraid. I believe that God is helping me to be strong. I trust him.

Write comments or draw. Use this verse: When? Where?

Scripture: Do not worry about tomorrow, for tomorrow will worry about itself. Each day has enough trouble of its own. Matthew 6:34 (NIV)

Nana's words: I can trust God to help me with any problems I may face today. Tomorrow, I believe he can help me again.

Write comments or draw. Use this verse: When? Where?

Forgive

Scripture: When you stand praying, if you hold anything against anyone, forgive them, so that your Father in heaven may forgive you your sins. Mark 11:25 (NIV)

Nana's words: I can choose to forgive people because I know God forgives me for the things I've done wrong. Giving others a blessing helps me to forgive them.

Write comments or draw. Use this verse: When? Where?

Scripture: Do not be overcome by evil, but overcome evil with good. Romans 12:21 (NIV)

Nana's words: I can bless people, so they are kind and honest. I can forgive others and myself.

Write comments or draw. Use this verse: When? Where?

Scripture: Then Peter came to him and asked, Sir, how many times shall I forgive a brother who sins against me? Seven times?

No! Jesus replied. Seventy times seven! Matthew 18:21 (TLB)

Nana's words: I can remember that God has forgiven me many, many times. So, I can forgive other people many, many times.

Write comments or draw. Use this verse: When? Where?

Scripture: Love your enemies and pray for those who persecute you. Matthew 5:43 (NIV)

Nana's words: When people are mean, I can ask God to bless them with kindness. I bless them, too. I can feel better when I pray and bless people who have hurt me.

Write comments or draw. Use this verse: When? Where?

Scripture: Be gentle and ready to forgive; never hold grudges. Remember, the Lord forgives you, so you must forgive others. Colossians 3:13 (TLB)

Nana's words: I can forgive myself, and I'm grateful that God removes guilt and shame. He forgives me. God's forgiveness helps me to forgive others.

Write comments or draw. Use this verse: When? Where?

Scripture: Jesus said, "Father, forgive them, for they don't know what they are doing." And the soldiers gambled for his clothes by throwing dice. Luke 23:34 (NLT)

Nana's words: I know Jesus forgave people who killed him. And I know Jesus can help me forgive people who hurt me.

Write comments or draw. Use this verse: When? Where?

Friends

Scripture: So, encourage each other and build each other up as you are already doing. 1 Thessalonians 5:11 (NLT)

Nana's words: I can encourage my friends to do the right things. Then my friends are more likely to encourage me.

Write comments or draw. Use this verse: When? Where?

Scripture: Just as iron sharpens iron; friends sharpen the minds of each other. Proverb 27:17 (CEV)

Nana's words: I can choose friends who are caring and forgiving, friends who are responsible and respectful. We can get smarter and stronger together. We can forgive each other when we make mistakes.

Write comments or draw. Use this verse: When? Where?

Scripture: There are "friends" who destroy each other, but a true friend sticks closer than a brother. Proverb 18:24 (NLT)

Nana's words: I can choose friends who stick with me during hard times. I can avoid people who act mean to me or tell lies about me. I can refuse to make fun of my friends.

Write comments or draw. Use this verse: When? Where?

Gossip

Scripture: Dishonest people use gossip to destroy their neighbors; good people are protected by their own good sense. Proverb 11:9 (CEV)

Nana's words: I can refuse to hurt people with gossip and mean words. God can give me wisdom and common sense to protect myself and others.

Write comments or draw. Use this verse: When? Where?

Scripture: A gossip betrays a confidence, but a trustworthy person keeps a secret. Proverb 11:13 (NIV)

Nana's words: I am a trustworthy person. I can keep a secret or ask people not to tell me their secrets.

Write comments or draw. Use this verse: When? Where?

Scripture: Don't say cruel things and don't tell lies. Psalm 34:13 (CEV)

Nana's words: Even if my friends say cruel things, I can refuse to do it, too. If someone says something that is a little bit true and a little bit false, I can refuse to be tricked. I can ask questions. I can listen for the whole truth.

Write comments or draw. Use this verse: When? Where?

Scripture: Kind words are good medicine, but deceitful words can really hurt. Proverb 15:4 (CEV)

Nana's words: I feel good when I speak kindly to others and myself. I know that exaggerating about weaknesses can hurt me or others. I can choose to use kind words.

Write comments or draw. Use this verse: When? Where?

Gratitude

Scripture: Say "thank you" to the Lord for being so good, for always being so loving and kind. Has the Lord redeemed you? Then speak out! Tell others he has saved you from your enemies. Psalm 107:1 (TLB)

Nana's words: I am grateful to God for his help and hope. I can tell others about his goodness and greatness.

Write comments or draw. Use this verse: When? Where?

Scripture: Give thanks to the Lord, call on his name; make known among the nations what he has done. Psalm 105:1 (NIV)

Nana's words: I can enjoy thanking God for all the wonderful things he does. I can share with people and tell them about God's love and kindness.

Write comments or draw. Use this verse: When? Where?

Scripture: Give thanks in all circumstances, for this is God's will for you in Christ Jesus. 1 Thessalonians 5:18 (NIV)

Nana's words: When I have problems or there are troubles around me, I can look for something to be thankful about. When I am grateful, I think more clearly and more creatively.

Write comments or draw. Use this verse: When? Where?

Greed

Scripture: Selfish people cause trouble, but you will live a full life if you trust the Lord. Proverb 28:25 (CEV)

Nana's words: I can refuse to be selfish. I can trust God and share. I know I can be happier.

Write comments or draw. Use this verse: When? Where?

Scripture: Then he said to the crowd, "Don't be greedy! Owning a lot of things won't make your life safe." Luke 12:15 (CEV)

Nana's words: I can listen to Jesus and refuse to be greedy. I know that having lots of things doesn't make me safe.

Write comments or draw. Use this verse: When? Where?

Scripture: Sometimes you can become rich by being generous or poor by being greedy. Proverb 11:24 (CEV)

Nana's words: I can be generous and feel good about myself. If I get rich, I can refuse to be greedy.

Write comments or draw. Use this verse: When? Where?

Health

Scripture: Is anyone among you sick? Let him call for the elders of the church, and let them pray over him, anointing him with oil in the name of the Lord. James 5:14 (ESV)

Nana's words: I can ask for prayers from people who love me or from people who have faith that God can help me. If my family or friends are sick, I can pray for them.

Write comments or draw. Use this verse: When? Where?

Scripture: He said to her, "Daughter, your faith has healed you. Go in peace and be freed from your suffering." Mark 5:34 (NIV)

Nana's words: I have faith, and I can believe that God can help me feel better. I can choose to think about Jesus' compassion. He said that faith can heal. I can trust God and do things to get well.

Write comments or draw. Use this verse: When? Where?

Scripture: Gentle words cause life and health; griping brings discouragement. Proverb 15:4 (TLB)

Nana's words: I can speak tenderly to myself when I'm sick. I encourage my body to heal. And I can firmly tell illness to go away. Kind words help me to feel loved and healthy. When I'm in pain, I can avoid thinking about things I can't do. I think about things that I *can* do. Even before I feel well, I can thank God for helping me.

Write comments or draw. Use this verse: When? Where?

Scripture: A cheerful heart is good like medicine. Proverb 17:22 (TLB)

Nana's words: I can smile and speak cheerfully. I can do healthy things to make me feel healthy and happy. Cheerfulness is like medicine, so I take it every day.

Write comments or draw. Use this verse: When? Where?

Scripture: Pleasant sights and good reports give happiness and health. Proverb 15:30 (TLB)

Nana's words: I can read good stories that encourage me. I look for good things that make me feel happy and healthy. I can choose to think about peaceful people, places, or things.

Write comments or draw. Use this verse: When? Where?

Help

Scripture: I lift up my eyes to the mountains – where does my help come from? My help comes from the Lord, the Maker of heaven and earth. Psalm 121:1 (NIV)

Nana's words: I can look to the mountains and the sky for God's greatness. I know that my help comes from God. He made heaven and earth. He can help me and direct me.

Write comments or draw. Use this verse: When? Where?

Scripture: God is our refuge and strength, always ready to help in times of trouble. Psalm 46:1 (NLT)

Nana's words: God is always ready to help me when I have problems. He helps me to be strong and safe. I can choose to be wise and talk with God.

Write comments or draw. Use this verse: When? Where?

Scripture: So do not fear, for I am with you; do not be dismayed, for I am your God. I can strengthen you and help you. I can uphold you with my righteous right hand. Isaiah 41:10 (NIV)

Nana's words: I can have courage because I know God is with me. He will give me strength and help me.

Write comments or draw. Use this verse: When? Where?

Honesty

Scripture: You will know the truth, and the truth will set you free. John 8:32 (ESV)

Nana's words: I know that speaking the truth can make me feel less anxious, angry, or guilty. But even if I can't tell the truth to anyone, I can tell God the truth. He will help me.

<u>Write comments or draw. Use this verse: When? Where?</u>

Scripture: Teach me your way, O Lord, that I may walk in your truth. Psalm 86:11 (ESV)

Nana's words: I can listen to what God teaches me. I am honest with myself and others.

<u>Write comments or draw. Use this verse: When? Where?</u>

Scripture: The Lord is near to all who call on him, to all who call on him in truth. Psalm 145:18 (ESV)

Nana's words: I honestly talk to God when I feel very upset. I remember that God is near me, and he can help. I ask God to help me know the truth about myself and others. If I've done something wrong, God can forgive me and bless me.

Write comments or draw. Use this verse: When? Where?

Hope

Scripture: We must hold tightly to the hope we say is ours. After all, we can trust the one who made the agreement with us. Hebrews 10:23 (CEV)

Nana's words: I can have hope and firmly hold onto it. I can refuse to be hopeless. I trust God who promises to help me. I can do what I know is right and good.

Write comments or draw. Use this verse: When? Where?

Scripture: With all my heart, I am waiting, Lord, for you! I trust your promises. Psalm 130:5 (CEV)

Nana's words: I can wait for God to help me. With all my heart, I can trust that he will help me.

Write comments or draw. Use this verse: When? Where?

Scripture: For I know the plans I have for you, declares the Lord, plans to prosper you and not to harm you, plans to give you hope and a future. Jeremiah 29:11 (NIV)

Nana's words: God says he has good plans for me. I can trust him to give me hope and help me now and later.

Write comments or draw. Use this verse: When? Where?

Scripture: Why, my soul, are you downcast? Why so disturbed within me? Put your hope in God, for I can yet praise him, my Savior and my God. Psalm 42:11 (NIV)

Nana's words: Why am I so unhappy? I can put my hope in God and praise him. I know he can help me. I can thank him now.

Write comments or draw. Use this verse: When? Where?

Scripture: Guide me in your truth and teach me, for you are God my Savior, and my hope is in you all day long. Psalm 25:5 (NIV)

Nana's words: I can trust God to teach me to be honest. During the day, I can often talk with him. He helps me when I have problems.

Write comments or draw. Use this verse: When? Where?

Scripture: His purpose was for the nations to seek after God and perhaps feel their way toward him and find him – though he is not far from any one of us. Acts 17:27 (NLT)

Nana's words: I can feel my way toward God. I can talk and act in ways that bring me closer to him. I can choose to be grateful because God is near me. I take time to talk with him.

Write comments or draw. Use this verse: When? Where?

Scripture: I pray that God, the source of hope, will fill you completely with joy and peace because you trust in him. Then you will overflow with confident hope through the power of the Holy Spirit. Romans 15:13 (NLT)

Nana's words: God is my source of hope. I can believe he will give me joy and peace because I talk to him and trust him.

Write comments or draw. Use this verse: When? Where?

Humility

Scripture: Humble yourselves before the Lord, and he will lift you up. James 4:10 (NIV)

Nana's words: I can be honest with God about myself. He makes me feel loved and encourages me. I don't have to show off.

Write comments or draw. Use this verse: When? Where?

Scripture: Live in harmony with one another. Do not be proud but be willing to associate with people of low position. Do not be conceited. Romans 12:16 (NIV)

Nana's words: I can be kind to others and take an interest in them. I look for their good qualities. I can be humble and honest about myself.

Write comments or draw. Use this verse: When? Where?

Scripture: The Lord God has told us what is right and what he demands: "See that justice is done, let mercy be your first concern, and humbly obey your God." Micah 6:8 (CEV)

Nana's words: I can choose to do what God said: Be kind. Be fair. Humbly obey God.

Write comments or draw. Use this verse: When? Where?

Scripture: Sitting down, Jesus called the Twelve and said, "Anyone who wants to be first must be the very last, and the servant of all." Mark 9:35 (NIV)

Nana's words: I like to be first, but it's better to help people. So, I will.

Write comments or draw. Use this verse: When? Where?

Scripture: Take my yoke upon you and learn from me, for I am gentle and humble in heart, and you will find rest for your souls. For my yoke is easy and my burden is light. Matthew 11:29 (NIV)

Nana's words: When I feel upset or very tired, I can talk to God and ask for help. He can help me to be gentle and humble. Then I can rest well.

<u>Write comments or draw. Use this verse: When? Where?</u>

Jealousy

Scripture: A peaceful heart leads to a healthy body; jealousy is like cancer in the bones. Proverb 14:30 (NIV)

Nana's words: I feel good when I act kindly and peacefully. I can refuse to be jealous. Jealousy is tricky. It makes me feel bad – sooner or later.

Write comments or draw. Use this verse: When? Where?

Scripture: Where you have envy and selfish ambition, there you find disorder and every evil practice. James 3:16 (NIV)

Nana's words: I can be generous with my words and actions. I can refuse to be selfish and jealous. I know that jealousy leads to other problems. And I don't want them.

Write comments or draw. Use this verse: When? Where?

Scripture: Do not envy the violent or choose any of their ways. For the Lord detests the perverse but take the upright into his confidence. Proverb 3:31 (NIV)

Nana's words: I can refuse to act mean or violent. When I do and say things that are good, I make God happy. And that can make me feel good.

Write comments or draw. Use this verse: When? Where?

Joy

Scripture: Those who listen to instruction will prosper; those who trust the Lord will be joyful. Proverb 16:20 (NLT)

Nana's words: I can trust God to help me listen to instructions. I practice listening, focusing and paying attention. When I do what God teaches, I can feel joyful.

Write comments or draw. Use this verse: When? Where?

Scripture: Let us come to him with thanksgiving. Let us sing psalms of praise to him. Psalm 95:2 (NLT)

Nana's words: I can talk to God and thank him. I can sing, hum, or whistle my little songs of thanksgiving. That can help me feel joyful.

Write comments or draw. Use this verse: When? Where?

Scripture: You have shown me the path to life, and you make me glad by being near to me. Sitting at your right side, I can always be joyful. Psalm 16:11 (CEV)

Nana's words: I can feel joyful when I talk to God. I know the way to a better life: Be kind, be fair, and walk humbly with God.

<u>Write comments or draw. Use this verse: When? Where?</u>

Scripture: Finally, brothers and sisters, whatever is true, whatever is noble, whatever is right, whatever is pure, whatever is lovely, whatever is admirable — if anything is excellent or praiseworthy — think about such things. Philippians 4:8 (NIV)

Nana's words: I can think about things that are good, fair, and kind. This helps me to feel joyful.

<u>Write comments or draw. Use this verse: When? Where?</u>

Scripture: His master said to him, "Well done, good and faithful servant. You have been faithful over a little; I can set you over much. Enter into the joy of your master." Matthew 25:23 (ESV)

Nana's words: I can use my skills and talents for good purposes. I am smart. I know what I need to do, and I can do it. This pleases God, and he will bless me. I can feel joyful.

__Write comments or draw. Use this verse: When? Where?__

Scripture: Rejoice always, pray continually, give thanks in all circumstances; for this is God's will for you in Jesus Christ. 1 Thessalonians 5:16 (NIV)

Nana's words: I can always be grateful for something, for any little thing. I can be grateful for special people, places, and things. I can thank God for any blessing in my life. Gratitude helps me feel joyful.

__Write comments or draw. Use this verse: When? Where?__

Scripture: Let all who take refuge in you rejoice; let them sing joyful praises forever. Spread your protection over them, that all who love your name may be filled with joy. Psalm 5:11 (NLT)

Nana's words: When I'm in trouble, I can talk to God and ask him for help or protection. Then I can sing, hum, or whistle songs to thank or praise God for his greatness.

Write comments or draw. Use this verse: When? Where?

Kindness

Scripture: Some people make cutting remarks, but the words of the wise bring healing. Proverb 12:18 (NLT)

Nana's words: I can speak lovingly and kindly to others and myself. I can refuse to be sarcastic and mean to my family, myself, or others. My kind words are soothing and healing. That can make me feel good.

Write comments or draw. Use this verse: When? Where?

Scripture: A man who is kind benefits himself, but a cruel man hurts himself. Proverb 11:17 (ESV)

Nana's words: I can be kind to others and myself. I can refuse to be mean. When I'm kind to others, I feel encouraged.

Write comments or draw. Use this verse: When? Where?

Scripture: Try to show as much compassion as your Father does. Never criticize or condemn, or it will all come back on you. Go easy on others; then they will do the same for you. Luke 6:36 (TLB)

Nana's words: God has compassion for me and others. I can refuse to act mean and criticize others or myself. I want people to be kind to me, so I can be kind to them.

<u>Write comments or draw. Use this verse: When? Where?</u>

Scripture: You must love God with all your heart, soul, mind, and strength. The second most important commandment says: "Love others as much as you love yourself. No other commandment is more important than these." Mark 12:31 (CEV)

Nana's words: With my heart, I can be grateful for God's compassion and love. With my mind, I can think about God's power and goodness; and I thank him. With my strength, I can do good things to help others and myself.

<u>Write comments or draw. Use this verse: When? Where?</u>

Scripture: Pleasant words are a honeycomb, sweet to the soul and healing to the bones. Proverb 16:24 (TLB)

Nana's words: I know that when I speak kindly to others and myself, I can feel calm and loving. I can be joyful.

<u>Write comments or draw. Use this verse: When? Where?</u>

Loneliness

Scripture: The Lord himself goes before you and will be with you. He will never leave you nor forsake you. Do not be afraid. Do not be discouraged. Deuteronomy 31:8 (NIV)

Nana's words: God will never leave me. He is with me all the time. If I feel afraid or discouraged, I can talk to God. I can ask for good friends.

Write comments or draw. Use this verse: When? Where?

Scripture: Even when I walk through the darkest valley, I can not be afraid, for you are close beside me. Your rod and your staff protect and comfort me. Psalm 23:4 (NLT)

Nana's words: Even when I feel lonely. I can remember God is with me. He comforts me and protects me. I can turn to him. I can look for good friends.

Write comments or draw. Use this verse: When? Where?

Scripture: The righteous cry out, and the Lord hears them. He delivers them from all their troubles. The Lord is close to the brokenhearted and saves those who are crushed in spirit. Psalm 34:17 (NIV)

Nana's words: When I feel sad or lonely, I can cry or talk to God. I remember that he hears me. He can help me find solutions for problems. I know that he is close to me and loves me.

Write comments or draw. Use this verse: When? Where?

Love

Scripture: Dear children, let's not merely say that we love each other. Let us show the truth by our actions. 1 John 3:18 (NLT)

Nana's words: I tell my family and friends that I love them. And I can do things to show my love for them.

<u>Write comments or draw. Use this verse: When? Where?</u>

Scripture: Love forgets mistakes; nagging about them parts the best of friends. Proverb 17:9 (TLB)

Nana's words: I love my family and friends. We can learn from our mistakes. I can refuse to nag and scold other people (or myself) about mistakes. We can encourage each other.

<u>Write comments or draw. Use this verse: When? Where?</u>

Scripture: Above all, love each other deeply, because love covers over a multitude of sins. 1 Peter 4:8 (NIV)

Nana's words: I can act and speak with love. Even when I have hurt others or myself, love helps to heal me or others. Love helps me feel God's forgiveness.

<u>Write comments or draw. Use this verse: When? Where?</u>

Scripture: Jesus replied: "You must love the Lord your God with all your heart, all your soul, and all your mind. This is the first and greatest commandment. A second is equally important: Love your neighbor as yourself. Matthew 22:37 (NLT)

Nana's words: I love God. I can love my neighbor. And I can love myself.

<u>Write comments or draw. Use this verse: When? Where?</u>

Your love for one another will prove to the world that you are my disciples. John 13:35 (NLT)

Nana's words: People will know that I love God by the way I show love to others.

<u>*Write comments or draw. Use this verse: When? Where?*</u>

Mistakes

Scripture: All of us do many wrong things. But if you can control your tongue, you are mature and able to control your whole body. James 3:2 (CEV)

Nana's words: We all make mistakes. I can refuse to be mean to myself. I can practice controlling what I say and do. I know God will help me. He forgives me. He can show me ways to change.

__Write comments or draw. Use this verse: When? Where?__

Scripture: So humble yourselves under the mighty power of God, and at the right time he will lift you up in honor. 1 Peter 5:6 (NLT)

Nana's words: I can be honest with God when I make mistakes. I can tell God my deepest secrets when I do something wrong. He will help me. He will forgive me.

__Write comments or draw. Use this verse: When? Where?__

Scripture: Surrender yourself to God! Resist the devil, and he will run from you. James 4:7 (CEV)

Nana's words: I can stop trying to solve problems all alone. I can ask God for help. I firmly refuse to do things I know are wrong and hurtful. Then temptation goes away.

<u>Write comments or draw. Use this verse: When? Where?</u>

Scripture: Put on all the armor that God gives, so you can defend yourself against the devil's tricks. Ephesians 6:11 (CEV)

Nana's words: I can do special things that protect me. I remember that God loves me. I can ask for help. I can tell the truth and act peacefully. I can use helpful Scripture verses and trust God. I thank God for what he's going to do.

<u>Write comments or draw. Use this verse: When? Where?</u>

Scripture: Don't be afraid. I am with you. Don't tremble with fear. I am your God. I can make you strong, as I protect you with my arm and give you victories. Isaiah 41:10 (CEV)

Nana's words: I know God can make me strong and help me to learn from my mistakes. I don't have to be afraid. I can think and look for solutions. God can help me through this.

Write comments or draw. Use this verse: When? Where?

Scripture: Love forgets mistakes; nagging about them parts the best of friends. Proverb 17:9 (TLB)

Nana's words: I love my family and friends. We learn from our mistakes. I can refuse to blame others for my actions. I can refuse to nag and scold other people (or myself) about mistakes. We can plan ways to change and encourage each other. We can love each other. Love helps us heal.

Write comments or draw. Use this verse: When? Where?

Obey

Scripture: My son, keep your father's command and do not forsake your mother's teaching. Proverb 6:20 (NIV)

Nana's words: I can obey my parents. I can practice doing the good things they teach me to do.

Write comments or draw. Use this verse: When? Where?

Scripture: Respect your father and your mother, and you will live a long time in the land I am giving you. Exodus 20:12 (CEV)

Nana's words: I can treat my parents with respect. I can refuse to be disrespectful. I plan ways to talk respectfully when I'm angry or upset me. This helps me feel happier and healthier.

Write comments or draw. Use this verse: When? Where?

Scripture: Anyone who listens to my teaching and follows it is wise, like a person who builds a house on solid rock. Matthew 7:24 (NLT)

Nana's words: I can practice what Jesus teaches me to do. Then I can be stronger and smarter when problems happen.

Write comments or draw. Use this verse: When? Where?

Scripture: When you obey me, you are living in my love, just as I obey my Father and live in his love. John 15:10 (TLB)

Nana's words: I can feel God's love for me when I do things that I know are good and right.

Write comments or draw. Use this verse: When? Where?

Scripture: Keep putting into practice all you learned and received from me – everything you heard from me and saw me doing. Then the God of peace will be with you. Philippians 4:9 (NLT)

Nana's words: I can practice acting with kindness and forgiveness. I can be honest and generous. These things help me to I feel God's peace.

Write comments or draw. Use this verse: When? Where?

Patience

Scripture: Controlling your temper is better than being a hero who captured a city. Proverb 16:32 (NLT)

Nana's words: I can control my temper. I know that patience is better than getting into fights. When I'm angry, I can take deep breaths and think before I speak.

Write comments or draw. Use this verse: When? Where?

Scripture: Whoever is patient has great understanding, but one who is quick-tempered displays folly. Proverb 14:29 (NIV)

Nana's words: I can be patient and think of ways to fix problems. I can ask for help. If I can't change something now, I can accept it. Maybe I can try again later.

Write comments or draw. Use this verse: When? Where?

Scripture: Let's not get tired of doing what is good. At just the right time, we will reap a harvest of blessing if we don't give up. Galatians 6:9 (NLT)

Nana's words: I can help people. I can do my chores and homework. I give myself compassion, but I don't give up. Then I can feel better and stronger.

Write comments or draw. Use this verse: When? Where?

Scripture: Since God chose you to be the holy people he loves, you must clothe yourself with tenderhearted mercy, kindness, humility, gentleness, and patience. Colossians 3:12 (NLT)

Nana's words: God loves me. He chose me to be fair and kind. He can help me to act with humility, gentleness, and patience. I know I'm loved.

Write comments or draw. Use this verse: When? Where?

Peer Pressure

Scripture: My child, if sinners entice you, turn your back on them! Proverb 1:10 (NLT)

Nana's words: If people try to get me to do something wrong, I can walk away. I plan ways to leave or to say no. I can make a list of ways to say no or to leave safely.

Write comments or draw. Use this verse: When? Where?

Scripture: Walk with the wise and become wise; associate with [foolish people] and get in trouble. Proverb 13:20 (NLT)

Nana's words: I can spend time with wise friends. I can stay away from people who like to do bad things. I encourage my friends to be kind.

Write comments or draw. Use this verse: When? Where?

Scripture: I'm not trying to win the approval of people, but of God. If pleasing people were my goal, I would not be Christ's servant. Galatians 1:10 (NLT)

Nana's words: I can get approval from God. I don't need the approval of people who say or do bad things. I know what's right and I can act kindly.

Write comments or draw. Use this verse: When? Where?

Scripture: Don't copy the behavior and customs of this world, but let God transform you into a new person by changing the way you think. Then you will learn to know God's will for you, which is good and pleasing and perfect. Romans 12:2 (NLT)

Nana's words: I can refuse to be mean and selfish. I don't copy people who are arrogant and lie. I practice acting kind and forgiving. I can feel good when I am honest and generous. God can change the way I think when I pray and listen to my conscience.

Write comments or draw. Use this verse: When? Where?

Scripture: The temptations in your life are no different from what others experience. And God is faithful. He will not allow the temptation to be more than you can stand. When you are tempted, he will show you a way out so that you can endure. 1 Corinthians 10:13 (NLT)

Nana's words: I know everyone gets tempted to do wrong things. When I'm tempted, I can look for ways to distract myself or get away. I can find ways to protect myself from temptation and problems.

Write comments or draw. Use this verse: When? Where?

Scripture: You must not follow the crowd in doing wrong. When you are called to testify in a dispute, do not be swayed by the crowd to twist justice. Exodus 23:2 (NLT)

Nana's words: I know what is right and wrong. I can refuse to follow people who lie, bully, or trick others. I can refuse to lie to myself or others.

Write comments or draw. Use this verse: When? Where?

Persist

Scripture: Let us not become weary in doing good, for at the proper time we will reap a harvest if we do not give up. Galatians 6:9 (NIV)

Nana's words: I can take a break, but I won't give up! I can refuse to quit. I have been strong and smart before. I can be strong and smart again. God helped me before, and he will help me again.

Write comments or draw. Use this verse: When? Where?

Scripture: I can do all things through him who gives me strength. Philippians 4:12 (NIV)

Nana's words: I *can* do all things with God's strength. When I need help, I can talk, cry, or write to God. I can imagine getting help from him and others. I can reach my goals.

Write comments or draw. Use this verse: When? Where?

Scripture: Be bold and strong! Banish fear and doubt! For remember, the Lord your God is with you wherever you go. Joshua 1:9 (TLB)

Nana's words: I am strong and courageous. I can refuse to be anxious about my work. I can remember God is with me. I can ask for help.

Write comments or draw. Use this verse: When? Where?

Scripture: Since we are surrounded by such a great cloud of witnesses, let us throw off everything that hinders and the sin that so easily entangles, and let us run with perseverance the race marked out for us. Hebrews 12:1 (NIV)

Nana's words: I can imagine persisting and reaching my goals. I can ignore distractions and things that make me lose my focus. God gave me a good purpose for my life. I can achieve it.

Write comments or draw. Use this verse: When? Where?

Scripture: Fight the good fight of faith. 1 Timothy 6:12 (NIV)

Nana's words: I imagine overcoming any obstacles that I may face today. I can choose to fight fear with faith and trust God.

Write comments or draw. Use this verse: When? Where?

Scripture: Keep on asking, and you will receive what you ask for. Keep on seeking, and you will find. Keep on knocking, and the door will be opened for you. For everyone who asks, receives. Everyone who seeks, find. And to everyone who knocks, the door will be opened. Matthew 7:7 (NLT)

Nana's words: I ask God for what I need. I can look for it. I can persist.

Write comments or draw. Use this verse: When? Where?

Praise

Scripture: Let everything that has breath praise the Lord. Praise the Lord. Psalm 150:6 (NIV)

Nana's words: I praise and thank God for his greatness and for all his creations. I can enjoy acting grateful.

Write comments or draw. Use this verse: When? Where?

Scripture: Praise the Lord. Give thanks to the Lord, for he is good! His faithful love endures forever. Psalm 106:1 (NLT)

Nana's words: I thank God because he is so good. He always loves me.

Write comments or draw. Use this verse: When? Where?

Scripture: Is anyone among you in trouble? Let him pray. Is anyone happy? Let him sing songs of praise. James 5:13 (NIV)

Nana's words: When I'm in trouble, I can pray. When I'm happy, I can praise God for his greatness and all his blessings.

Write comments or draw. Use this verse: When? Where?

Scripture: I can keep on hoping for your help; I can praise you more and more. Psalm 71:14 (NLT)

Nana's words: I know God will help me now or later. Even before I get help, I can thank God and praise him. Then I'll be more aware of his help.

Write comments or draw. Use this verse: When? Where?

Rest

Scripture: Rest in the Lord; wait patiently for him to act. Psalm 37:7 (TLB)

Nana's words: I can breathe deeply and rest. I imagine God is with me. I trust him to help me as I solve my problems after I rest.

Write comments or draw. Use this verse: When? Where?

Scripture: It is useless for you to work so hard from early morning until late at night, anxiously working for food to eat; for God gives rest to his loved ones. Psalm 127:2 (NLT)

Nana's words: I can take little breaks in the day and rest at night. I can refuse to worry, but I can think of possible solutions. I know God can help me sleep at night and do my work in the morning.

Write comments or draw. Use this verse: When? Where?

Scripture: By the seventh day God had finished the work he had been doing; so, on the seventh day he rested from all his work. Genesis 2:2 (NIV)

Nana's words: At the end of the week, I get a day to rest. I can finish my work early so I can relax for a whole day.

Write comments or draw. Use this verse: When? Where?

Scripture: Come to me, all you who are weary and burdened, and I can give you rest. Take my yoke upon you and learn from me, for I am gentle and humble in heart, and you will find rest for your souls. For my yoke is easy and my burden is light. Matthew 11:28 (NIV)

Nana's words: I can imagine giving God all my worries and problems. God teaches me to be wise, honest, and forgiving. He helps me to be gentle and rest.

Write comments or draw. Use this verse: When? Where?

Scripture: My presence will go with you, and I can give you rest. Exodus 33:14 (NIV)

Nana's words: I can picture God near me as I rest. He can help me sleep and restore my energy.

Write comments or draw. Use this verse: When? Where?

Revenge

Scripture: Don't mistreat someone who has mistreated you. But try to earn the respect of others. Romans 12:17 (CEV)

Nana's words: I can be respectful. I can refuse to hurt someone who has hurt me. Instead, I ask God to help them act kind to me and others.

Write comments or draw. Use this verse: When? Where?

Scripture: Do not seek revenge or bear a grudge against anyone among your people, but love your neighbor as yourself. I am the Lord. Leviticus 19:18 (NIV)

Nana's words: I can pray for people who hurt me or bless them with kindness for me and others. I treat myself with respect and kindness.

Write comments or draw. Use this verse: When? Where?

Scripture: But when you are praying, first forgive anyone you are holding a grudge against, so that your Father in heaven will forgive your sins, too. Mark 11:25 (NLT)

Nana's words: Sometimes, I think I can't forgive. But God has forgiven me many, many times. So, I can forgive others and bless them, too.

Write comments or draw. Use this verse: When? Where?

Sadness

Scripture: Even when I walk through the darkest valley, I can not be afraid, for you are close beside me. Your rod and your staff protect and comfort me. Psalm 23:4 (NLT)

Nana's words: When I feel sad and lonely, I can remember God is with me. He comforts me and protects me. I can turn to him.

Write comments or draw. Use this verse: When? Where?

Scripture: Blessed are those who mourn, for they will be comforted. Matthew 5:4 (NIV)

Nana's words: Even though I am sad, I know God is here to comfort me. He will bless me and help me. I can remember that love never ends. There is hope, and I can find it.

Write comments or draw. Use this verse: When? Where?

Scripture: The righteous cry out, and the Lord hears them. He delivers them from all their troubles. The Lord is close to the brokenhearted and saves those who are crushed in spirit. Psalm 34:17 (NIV)

Nana's words: When I feel sad or lonely, I can cry or talk to God. I can remember that he hears me. He helps me find solutions for problems. I know that he is close to me and loves me.

<ins>Write comments or draw. Use this verse: When? Where?</ins>

Scripture: The Lord himself goes before you and will be with you. He will never leave you nor forsake you. Do not be afraid. Do not be discouraged. Deuteronomy 31:8 (NIV)

Nana's words: God will never leave me. He is with me all the time. He is with me when I'm sad. If I feel afraid or discouraged, I can talk to God.

<ins>Write comments or draw. Use this verse: When? Where?</ins>

School

Scripture: Work hard so you can present yourself to God and receive his approval. Be a good worker, one who does not need to be ashamed and who correctly explains the word of truth. 2 Timothy 2:15 (NLT)

Nana's words: I can study and do my work. I can ask for help when I need it. I can refuse to be ashamed of mistakes. I learn from my mistakes. I am smart.

Write comments or draw. Use this verse: When? Where?

Scripture: Encourage each other and build each other up, just as you are already doing. 1 Thessalonians 5:11 (NLT)

Nana's words: Encouragement helps me to learn faster and remember more. I encourage myself and others. I can choose to be kind to myself when I'm learning something new. I can take time to learn.

Write comments or draw. Use this verse: When? Where?

Scripture: Whatever you have learned or received or heard from me or seen in me – put it into practice. And the God of peace will be with you. Philippians 4:9 (NIV)

Nana's words: I can do the good things I have learned. I talk about them. I write or sing or dance about them. Practicing can help me to remember more.

Write comments or draw. Use this verse: When? Where?

Self-Compassion

Scripture: Gracious words are like a honeycomb, sweetness to the soul and health to the body. Proverb 16:24 (ESV)

Nana's words: I know God gives me grace. I can speak gracefully and kindly to myself or others. Kindness helps me feel healthy.

Write comments or draw. Use this verse: When? Where?

Scripture: Don't you realize that your body is the temple of the Holy Spirit, who lives in you and was given to you by God? 1 Corinthians 6:19 (NLT)

Nana's words: I know God is with me. I can respect myself and my body. I can take care of my body and my things. I try to stay healthy.

Write comments or draw. Use this verse: When? Where?

Scripture: You shall love the Lord your God with all your heart and with all your soul and with all your strength and with all your mind, and love your neighbor as yourself. Luke 10:27 (NIV)

Nana's words: I know the greatest commandment is to love and respect God, others and myself. I can trust God to help me have compassion for others and myself. That's God's will for me.

Write comments or draw. Use this verse: When? Where?

Self-Control

Scripture: Encourage the young men to be self-controlled. Titus 2:6 (NIV)

Nana's words: I can encourage myself and others to be self-controlled. We can support each other.

Write comments or draw. Use this verse: When? Where?

Scripture: For God gave us a spirit *not* of fear but of power and love and self-control. 2 Timothy 1:7 (ESV)

Nana's words: I don't have to be afraid. I can use the power, love, and self-control that God has given me. I can say "NO!" to things that hurt me or others.

Write comments or draw. Use this verse: When? Where?

Scripture: All athletes are disciplined in their training. They do it to win a prize that will fade away, but we do it for an eternal prize. So, I run with purpose in every step. 1 Corinthians 9:25 (NLT)

Nana's words: I can have self-control. I get lots of benefits from having self-control. Some of those benefits happen right now, others happen later. I can train myself to focus and listen. I can learn, step by step.

Write comments or draw. Use this verse: When? Where?

Scripture: God's Spirit makes us loving, happy, peaceful, patient, kind, good, faithful, gentle, and self-controlled. There is no law against behaving in any of these ways. Galatians 5:22 (CEV)

Nana's words: God has given me kindness, joy, and peace. I can believe he has blessed me with patience, goodness, and gentleness. I can talk and act with self-control.

Write comments or draw. Use this verse: When? Where?

Self-Esteem

Scripture: Thank you for making me so wonderfully complex! Your workmanship is marvelous – how well I know it. Psalm 139:14 (NLT)

Nana's words: God has made me in a special way. I can be grateful that I am unique. God has a special purpose for my life.

Write comments or draw. Use this verse: When? Where?

Scripture: The second most important commandment is like this one. And it is, "Love others as much as you love yourself" Matthew 22:39 (CEV)

Nana's words: I can respect myself and act kindly. When I am kind to myself, it is easier to treat others with kindness and respect.

Write comments or draw. Use this verse: When? Where?

Scripture: But the Lord told him, "Samuel don't think Eliab is the one just because he's tall and handsome. He isn't the one I've chosen. People judge others by what they look like, but I judge people by what is in their hearts." 1 Samuel 16:7 (CEV)

Nana's words: I am grateful that God cares about goodness and love. He doesn't care about people's looks. He cares about how people act and talk and think.

Write comments or draw. Use this verse: When? Where?

Scripture: For I know the plans I have for you, says the Lord. They are plans for good and not for disaster, to give you a future and a hope. Jeremiah 29:11 (NLT)

Nana's words: I can believe God has good plans for my life. I may not know them now, but I can trust God for my future. I can do the work I need to do now.

Write comments or draw. Use this verse: When? Where?

Shame

Scripture: If we confess our sins to God, he can always be trusted to forgive us and take our sins away. 1 John 1:9 (CEV)

Nana's words: I can tell God when I've done something wrong. I can trust him to forgive me. Then I can refuse to be ashamed.

Write comments or draw. Use this verse: When? Where?

Scripture: O Lord, you are so good, so ready to forgive, so full of unfailing love for all who ask for your help. Psalm 86:5 (NLT)

Nana's words: I can talk to God about my mistakes. I am so thankful that God loves me and forgives me.

Write comments or draw. Use this verse: When? Where?

Scripture: They say hurtful things, and they lie to people who want to live in peace. Psalm 35:20 (CEV)

Nana's words: I want to live in peace. I can refuse to be mean. If I hear lies about myself or others, I can refuse to believe them. I can tell myself and others the truth.

Write comments or draw. Use this verse: When? Where?

Share

Scripture: Share with the Lord's people who are in need. Practice hospitality. Romans 12:13 (NIV)

Nana's words: I can be friendly and generous when people come to my home. I can share with people. Acting kind makes me feel good. I know God blesses me for sharing with people in need.

Write comments or draw. Use this verse: When? Where?

Scripture: Don't forget to do good and to share with those in need. These are the sacrifices that please God. Hebrews 13:16 (NLT)

Nana's words: I can remember to act kind and share with people. I know that sharing makes God happy.

Write comments or draw. Use this verse: When? Where?

Scripture: Share each other's burdens, and in this way obey the law of Christ. If you think you are too important to help someone, you are only fooling yourself. Galatians 6:2 (NLT)

Nana's words: I can be kind to people when they are sad or upset. I feel happier when I obey God.

Write comments or draw. Use this verse: When? Where?

Scripture: If you give to others, you will be given a full amount in return. It will be packed down, shaken together, and spilling over into your lap. The way you treat others is the way you will be treated. Luke 6:38 (CEV)

Nana's words: I want to be treated with kindness and generosity. So, I can treat others that way.

Write comments or draw. Use this verse: When? Where?

Unfairness

Scripture: Learn to do good. Seek justice. Help the oppressed. Defend the cause of the orphans. Fight for the rights of widows. Isaiah 1:17 (NLT)

Nana's words: When someone has been unfair, I can use my anger to think of ways to solve the problem. I can ask for help.

Write comments or draw. Use this verse: When? Where?

Scripture: Don't be hateful and insult people just because they are hateful and insult you. Instead, treat everyone with kindness. You are God's chosen ones, and he will bless you. 1 Peter 3:9 (CEV)

Nana's words: I don't like when people are unfair. So, I can refuse to act unfair. I can choose to act kindly. I know God will bless me now or later.

Write comments or draw. Use this verse: When? Where?

Scripture: You must not follow the crowd in doing wrong. When you are called to testify in a dispute, do not be swayed by the crowd to twist justice. Exodus 23:2 (NLT)

Nana's words: I know what is right and wrong. I can refuse to be confused. I can refuse to lie myself. If someone tries to trick me or scare me, I can do things to stay safe.

Write comments or draw. Use this verse: When? Where?

Scripture: Jesus said, "Father, forgive them, for they don't know what they are doing." And the soldiers gambled for his clothes by throwing dice. Luke 23:34 (NLT)

Nana's words: I know Jesus forgave people who killed him. And I know Jesus can help me forgive people who are unfair to me.

Write comments or draw. Use this verse: When? Where?

The Lord's Prayer

Older version:

This, then, is how you should pray: Our Father in heaven, hallowed be your name, your kingdom come, your will be done, on earth as it is in heaven. Give us today our daily bread. And forgive us our debts, as we also have forgiven our debtors. And lead us not into temptation, but deliver us from the evil one. Matthew 6:9-13 (NIV)

Newer version:

You should pray like this: Our Father in heaven. Help us to honor your name. Come and set up your kingdom, so that everyone on earth will obey you, as you are obeyed in heaven. Give us our food for today. Forgive us for doing wrong, as we forgive others. Keep us from being tempted and protect us from evil. Matthew 6:9-13 (CEV)

Write comments or draw. Use this verse: When? Where?

·

Prayer for Peace

Lord, make me an instrument of your peace.

Where there is hatred, let me bring love.

Where there is offence, let me bring pardon.

Where there is discord, let me bring union.

Where there is error, let me bring truth.

Where there is doubt, let me bring faith.

Where there is despair, let me bring hope.

Where there is darkness, let me bring your light.

Where there is sadness, let me bring joy.

O Master, let me not seek as much to be consoled as to console,

to be understood as to understand,

to be loved as to love,

for it is in giving that one receives,

it is in self-forgetting that one finds,

it is in pardoning that one is pardoned,

it is in dying that one is raised to eternal life.

God bless you, my dears.

Love always,

Nana ♡

Do it Yourself

Want to find more Bible verses on specific topics?

Go to OpenBible.com. Click Topical. Type your question into the search bar.

Want to find various versions of the same Bible verse?

Go to BibleHub.com. Type the chapter and verse of the Scripture in the search bar. You'll find a long list of modern and classic translations for each Bible verse. Keep looking and you'll find the context of the verse. Read and learn more.

Hope Helps, from Nana

Made in the USA
Monee, IL
24 February 2023

27838345R00075